Pearl E. Dorn
Xmas gift
money! 1989.

To See a World
in a Grain of Sand

To See a World in a Grain of Sand

By Caesar Johnson

photographs by Edward Richardson III

Published by The C. R. Gibson Company

Contents

To see a world in a grain of sand
And a heaven in a wildflower:
Hold infinity in the palm of your hand,
And eternity in an hour.

William Blake

Being and
Becoming

Life is not a having and a getting,
but a being and a becoming.

Matthew Arnold

Doubt whom you will, but never yourself.

Christian Bovee

Every human being is intended to have a character of his own;
to be what no other is, and to do what no other can do.

William Channing

No one can give you better advice than yourself.

Cicero

Height

When I was young I felt so small
And frightened for the world was tall.

And even grasses seemed to me
A forest of immensity.

Until I learned that I could grow,
A glance would leave them far below.

Spanning a tree's height with my eye,
Suddenly I soared as high,

And fixing on a star I grew,
I pushed my head against the blue!

Still, like a singing lark, I find
Rapture to leave the grass behind.

And sometimes standing in a crowd
My lips are cool against a cloud.

Anne Morrow Lindbergh

A Lazy Thought

There go the grownups
To the office,
To the store.
Subway rush,
Traffic crush;
Hurry, scurry,
Worry, flurry.

No wonder
Grownups
Don't grow up
Any more.

It takes a lot
Of slow
To grow.

Eve Merriam

And only when we are no longer afraid do we begin to live
in every experience, painful or joyous; to live in gratitude
for every moment, to live abundantly.

Dorothy Thompson

No coward soul is mine,
No trembler in the world's storm-troubled
  sphere:
I see Heaven's glories shine,
And faith shines equal, arming me from fear.

Emily Brontë

What you can become, you are already.

Friedrich Hebbel

One who fears limits his activities. Failure is only the opportunity
to more intelligently begin again.

Henry Ford

It is difficulties that show what men are.

Epictetus

Wealth consists not in having great possessions,
but in having few wants.

Epicurus

Do You Fear The Wind?

Do you fear the force of the wind,
The slash of the rain?
Go face them and fight them,
Be savage again.
Go hungry and cold like the wolf,
Go wade like the crane:
The palms of your hands will thicken,
The skin of your cheek will tan,
You'll grow ragged and weary and swarthy,
But you'll walk like a man!

Hamlin Garland

Happiness? It is an illusion to think that more comfort means
more happiness. Happiness comes of the capacity to feel
deeply, to enjoy simply, to think freely, to risk life, to be needed.

Storm Jameson

God gives every bird his food,
but He does not throw it into the nest.

Josiah Gilbert Holland

What you think of yourself is much more
important than what others think of you.

Seneca

No man can produce great things who is not
thoroughly sincere in dealing with himself.

James Russell Lowell

This Is My Rock

This is my rock
And here I run
To steal the secret of the sun;

This is my rock
And here come I
Before the night has swept the sky;

This is my rock,
This is the place
I meet the evening face to face.

David McCord

The Angel that presided o'er my birth
Said, "Little creature, form'd of joy and mirth,
Go, love without the help of any thing on earth."

William Blake

Let us be of good cheer, however, remembering that the
misfortunes hardest to bear are those which never come.

James Russell Lowell

It is foolish to tear one's hair in grief as though
sorrow would be made less by baldness.

Cicero

A big dog saw a little dog chasing its tail and asked,
"Why are you chasing your tail so?" Said the puppy,
"I have mastered philosophy; I have solved the problems of the
universe which no dog before me has rightly solved; I have
learned that the best thing for a dog is happiness, and that happiness
is my tail. Therefore I am chasing it; and when I catch it
I shall have happiness."

Said the old dog, "My son, I, too, have paid attention to the
problems of the universe in my weak way, and I have formed
some opinions. I, too, have judged that happiness is a fine thing
for a dog, and that happiness is in my tail. But I have noticed
that when I chase after it, it keeps running away from me, but when
I go about my business, it comes after me."

C. L. James

Our greatest glory consists not in never falling,
but in rising every time we fall.

Oliver Goldsmith

Life consists not in holding good cards
but in playing those you do hold well.

Josh Billings

No man who has wrestled with a self-adjusting card table
can ever be quite the man he once was.

James Thurber

Unless you find some sort of loyalty, you cannot
find unity and peace in your active living.

Josiah Royce

Happiness is the sense that one matters.

Samuel Shoemaker

If you ever find happiness by hunting for it, you will find it as the old woman did her lost spectacles — on her own nose all the time.

Josh Billings

We have forty million reasons for failure,
but not a single excuse.

Rudyard Kipling

The Kingdom Of Man

Our world is the world within,
    Our life is the thought we take,
And never an outer sin
    Can mar it or break.

Brood not on the rich man's land,
    Sigh not for the miser's gold,
Holding in reach of your hand
    The treasure untold.

That lies in the Mines of Heart,
    That rest in the soul alone —
Bid worry and care depart,
    Come into your own!

John Kendrick Bangs

The only competition worthy of a wise man is with himself.

Washington Allston

Every man has three characters — that which he exhibits, that which he has, and that which he thinks he has.

Alphonse Karr

Even a fool, when he holdeth his peace, is counted wise.

Proverbs 17:28

Hit the ball over the fence and you can take
your time going around the bases.

John W. Raper

Don't refuse to go on an occasional wild-goose chase;
that is what wild geese are made for.

Henry S. Haskins

The best lightning rod for your protection is your own spine.

Ralph Waldo Emerson

One of the rarest things that man ever does is to do the best he can.

Josh Billings

Contentment

When spring arrives and lilacs blow
I'm not compelled to shovel snow.
In summer no one bothers me
To feed the fire, nor skate, nor ski.
In autumn no one longer needs
To waste the morning pulling weeds.
And winter brings no dewy dawn
When I must rise to mow the lawn.

So I am glad the seasons through
For what I do not have to do.

Arthur Guiterman

However mean your life is, meet it and live it; do not shun it
and call it hard names. It is not so bad as you are. It looks poorest
when you are richest. The fault-finder will find faults even in
paradise. Love your life.

Henry Thoreau

Being and Becoming 15

Rejoiceth not in iniquity, but rejoiceth in the truth;

Beareth all things, believeth all things, hopeth all things, endureth all things.

Charity never faileth: but whether there be prophecies, they shall fail; whether there be tongues, they shall cease; whether there be knowledge, it shall vanish away.

For we know in part, and we prophesy in part.

But when that which is perfect is come, then that which is in part shall be done away.

When I was a child, I spake as a child, I understood as a child, I thought as a child; but when I became a man, I put away childish things.

For now we see through a glass, darkly; but then face to face: now I know in part; but then shall I know even as also I am known.

And now abideth faith, hope, charity, these three; but the greatest of these is charity.

I Corinthians 13:6-13

No persons are more frequently wrong, than those who will not admit that they are wrong.

François, Duc de La Rochefoucauld

A sound discretion is not so much indicated by never making a mistake as by never repeating it.

Christian Bovee

When the fight begins within himself, A man's worth something.

Robert Browning

The most difficult secret for a man to keep is his own opinion of himself.

Marcel Pagnol

My code of life and conduct is simply this: work hard;
play to the allowable limit; disregard equally the good and bad
opinion of others; never do a friend a dirty trick . . . never grow
indignant over anything . . . live the moment to the utmost of its
possibilities . . . and be satisfied with life always, but never
with oneself.

George Jean Nathan

We make our fortunes and we call them fate.

Benjamin Disraeli

To get out of a difficulty go through it.

Samuel Easton

The optimist is the kind of person who believes
a housefly is looking for a way out.

George Jean Nathan

Be not simply good — be good for something.

Henry Thoreau

Little minds are tamed and subdued by misfortune,
but great minds rise above it.

Washington Irving

Put an end once and for all to this discussion
of what a good man should be, and be one.

Marcus Aurelius

A man should never be ashamed to say he has been wrong,
which is but saying in other words that he is wiser today than
he was yesterday.

Alexander Pope

All Things
Great and Small

He prayeth well, who loveth well
Both man and bird and beast.

He prayeth best who loveth best
All things both great and small;
For the dear God who loveth us,
He made and loveth all.

Samuel Taylor Coleridge

To me every hour of the light and dark is a miracle,
Every cubic inch of space is a miracle,
Every square yard of the surface of the earth is spread with the same,
Every foot of the interior swarms with the same.
To me the sea is a continual miracle,
The fishes that swim — the rocks — the motion of the waves —
    the ships with men in them.
What stranger miracles are there?

Walt Whitman

Look!

I eat from the dish of the world
    Trees, fields, flowers.
I drink from the glass of space
    Blue sea, sky.

I pour the sky over me
    In blue showers.
Look! I light up the day
    With my eye.

John Smith

The pleasantest things in the world are pleasant thoughts;
and the art of life is to have as many of them as possible.

Michel de Montaigne

April

It's lemonade, it's lemonade, it's daisy.
It's a roller-skating, scissor-grinding day;
It's gingham-waisted, chocolate flavored, lazy,
With the children flower-scattered at their play.

It's the sun like watermelon,
And the sidewalks overlaid
With a glaze of yellow yellow
Like a jar of marmalade.

It's the mower gently mowing,
And the stars like startled glass,
While the mower keeps on going
Through a waterfall of grass.

Then the rich magenta evening
Like a sauce upon the walk,
And the porches softly swinging
With a hammockful of talk.

It's the hobo at the corner
With his lilac-sniffing gait,
And the shy departing thunder
Of the fast departing skate.

It's lemonade, it's lemonade, it's April!
A water sprinkler, puddle winking time,
When a boy who peddles slowly, with a smile remote and holy,
Sells you April chocolate flavored for a dime.

Marcia Masters

God has put something noble and good
into every heart His hand created.

Mark Twain

We are but the ephemera of the moment, the brief custodians
of redwoods, which were ancient when Christ was born,
and of the birds of the air and animals of the forest which have
been evolving for countless millenniums. We do not own
the land we abuse, or the lakes and streams we pollute or
the raccoons and the otters which we persecute. Those who play
God in destroying any form of life are tampering with a
master plan too intricate for any of us to understand.

Sterling North

Never lose an opportunity of seeing anything that is beautiful;
for beauty is God's handwriting — a wayside sacrament

Ralph Waldo Emerson

Swift Things Are Beautiful

Swift things are beautiful:
Swallows and deer,
And lightning that falls
Bright-veined and clear,
Rivers and meteors,
Wind in the wheat,
The strong-withered horse,
The runners' sure feet.

And slow things are beautiful:
The closing of day,
The pause of the wave
That curves downward to spray
The ember that crumbles,
The opening flower,
And the ox that moves on
In the quiet of power.

Elizabeth Coatsworth

All Things Great and Small 21

I looked up and saw a squirrel jump from one high tree to another. He appeared to be aiming for a limb so far out of reach that the leap looked like suicide. He missed — but landed, safe and unconcerned, on a branch several feet lower. Then he climbed to his goal, and all was well.

An old man sitting on the bench said, "Funny, I've seen hundreds of 'em jump like that, especially when there are dogs around and they can't come to the ground. A lot of 'em miss, but I've never seen any hurt in trying." Then he chuckled. "I guess they've got to risk it if they don't want to spend their lives in one tree."

I thought, "A squirrel takes a chance — have I less nerve than a squirrel?"

Since then, whenever I have to choose between risking a new venture or hanging back, I hear the old man on the park bench saying, "They've got to risk it if they don't want to spend their lives in one tree."

So I've jumped again and again. And in jumping I've learned why the squirrels so often do it: it's fun.

Oscar Schisgall

If I can stop one Heart from breaking
I shall not live in vain
If I can ease one Life the Aching
Or cool one Pain

Or help one fainting Robin
Unto his Nest again
I shall not live in Vain.

Emily Dickinson

Pleasure is very seldom found where it is sought. Our brightest blazes of gladness are commonly kindled by unexpected sparks.

Samuel Johnson

Love all God's creation, the whole and every grain of sand in it.
Love every leaf, every ray of God's light. Love the animals,
love the plants, love everything. If you love everything, you will
perceive the divine mystery in things. Once you perceive it,
you will begin to comprehend it better every day. And you will come
at last to love the whole world with an all-embracing love.

Feodor Dostoyevsky

To Look at Any Thing

To look at any thing,
If you would know that thing,
You must look at it long:
To look at this green and say
'I have seen spring in these
Woods,' will not do — you must
Be the thing you see:
You must be the dark snakes of
Stems and ferny plumes of leaves,
You must enter in
To the small silences between
The leaves,
You must take your time
And touch the very peace
They issue from.

John Moffitt

The works of the Magician of the Beautiful are not like ours
and in the least fragment His artistry is no less present than in
the stars. We may enter the infinite through the minute no less
than through contemplation of the vast.

A.E.
(George William Russell)

Aristocracy

The Pedigree of Honey
  Does not concern the Bee —
A Clover, any time, to him
  Is Aristocracy.

Emily Dickinson

Give me no more than homely words,
And kindly thoughts, to build my house;
No more than what is given the birds
Or less than might be loaned a mouse.

Robert Nathan

God writes the gospel not in the Bible alone,
but on trees, and flowers, and clouds, and stars.

Martin Luther

Leavetaking

Vacation is over;
It's time to depart.
I must leave behind
(although it breaks my heart)

Tadpoles in the pond,
A can of eels,
A leaky rowboat,
Abandoned car wheels;

For I'm packing only
Necessities:
A month of sunsets
And two apple trees.

Eve Merriam

Wonder Wander

in the afternoon the children walk like ducks
like geese
like from here to there
eyeing bird-trees puppy dogs candy windows
sun balls ice cream wagons
lady bugs rose bushes fenced yards vacant lots
tall buildings
and other things
big business men take big business walks
wear big business clothes
carry big business briefcases talk about
big business affairs in
big business voices
young girls walk pretty on the streets
stroll the avenues linger by
shop windows wedding rings lady hats
shiny dresses fancy shoes
whisper like turkey hens passing the time
young men stride on parade dream headed
wild eyed eating up the world
with deep glances rubbing empty fingers
in their empty pockets and
planning
me, I wander around soft-shoed easy-legged
watching the scene as it goes
finding things sea-gull feathers pink baby roses
every time I see a letter on the sidewalk
I stop and look it might be
      for me

                      Lenore Kandel

It is great to be great, but it is greater to be human.

                      Will Rogers

Give Me Hills
to Climb

Hills

I never loved your plains,
   Your gentle valleys,
Your drowsy country lanes
   And pleached alleys.

I want my hills — the trail
   That scorns the hollow —
Up, up the ragged shale
   Where few will follow.

Up, over wooded crest,
   And mossy boulder,
With strong thigh, heaving chest,
   And swinging shoulder.

So let me hold my way,
   By nothing halted,
Until, at close of day,
   I stand exalted.

High on my hills of dream —
   Dear hills that know me!
And then how fair will seem
   The land below me!

How pure, at vesper-time
   The far bells chiming!
God, give me hills to climb
   And strength for climbing!

Arthur Guiterman

We never become truly spiritual by sitting down and wishing to become so. You must undertake something so great that you cannot accomplish it unaided.

Phillips Brooks

What on earth would a man do with himself
if something did not stand in his way?

H. G. Wells

Nothing will ever be attempted if all
possible objections must be first overcome.

Samuel Johnson

A ship in harbour is safe, but that is not
what ships are built for.

William Shedd

Life's a pretty precious and wonderful thing. You can't sit down
and let it lap around you . . . you have to plunge into it;
you have to dive through it! And you can't save it, you can't
store it up; you can't horde it in a vault. You've got to taste
it; you've got to use it. The more you use the more you have . . .
that's the miracle of it!

Kyle Samuel Crichton

Youth

We have tomorrow
Bright before us
Like a flame.

Yesterday
A night-gone thing,
A sun-down name.

And dawn-today
Broad arch above the road we came.

We march!

Langston Hughes

Never stand begging for that which you have the power to earn.

Miguel de Cervantes

Every individual has a place to fill in the world, and is important in some respect whether he chooses to be so or not.

Nathaniel Hawthorne

Whatever you are by nature, keep to it; never desert your line of talent. Be what nature intended you for, and you will succeed.

Sydney Smith

A man always has two reasons for doing anything — a good reason and the real reason.

J. P. Morgan

If thou of all thy mortal goods bereft
And from thy store alone two loaves are left,
Sell, sell thou one. Then with thy toll
Buy hyacinth — and speed thy soul.

Muslik-ud-Din

I find the great thing in this world is not so much where we stand, as in what direction we are moving.

Oliver Wendell Holmes

Finally whether you are citizens of America or citizens of the world, ask of us here the same high standards of strength and sacrifice which we ask of you. With a good conscience our only sure reward, with history the final judge of our deeds, let us go forth to lead the land we love, asking His blessing and His help, but knowing that here on earth God's work must truly be our own.

John F. Kennedy

There is no finer sensation in life than that which comes with victory over one's self. It feels good to go fronting into a hard wind, winning against its power; but it feels a thousand times better to go forward to a goal of inward achievement, brushing aside all your old internal enemies as you advance.

Vash Young

People are always blaming their circumstances for what they are. I don't believe in circumstances. The people who get on in this world are the people who get up and look for the circumstances they want, and if they can't find them, make them.

George Bernard Shaw

Self-knowledge is best learned, not by contemplation, but action. Strive to do your duty, and you will soon discover of what stuff you are made.

Johann Wolfgang von Goethe

Kindly Unhitch That Star, Buddy

I hardly suppose I know anybody who wouldn't rather be a
    success than a failure,
Just as I suppose every piece of crabgrass in the garden
    would much rather be an azalea,
And in celestial circles all the run-of-the-mill angels
    would rather be archangels or at least cherubim and
    seraphim.
And in the legal world all the little process-servers
    hope to grow up into great big bailiffim and sheriffim.
Indeed, everybody wants to be a wow,
But not everybody knows exactly how.
Some people think they will eventually wear diamonds
    instead of rhinestones

Only by everlastingly keeping their noses to their grhinestones,
And other people think they will be able to put in more
    time at Palm Beach and the Ritz
By not paying too much attention to attendance at the office
    but rather in being brilliant by starts and fits.
Some people after a full day's work sit up all night getting
    a college education by correspondence,
While others seem to think they'll get just as far by
    devoting their evenings to the study of the difference in
    temperament between brunettance and blondance.
Some stake their all on luck,
And others put their faith in their ability to pass the buck.
In short, the world is filled with people trying to achieve
    success,
And half of them think they'll get it by saying No and
    half of them by saying Yes.
And if all the ones who say No said Yes, and vice versa,
    such is the fate of humanity that ninety-nine per cent of
    them still wouldn't be any better off than they were before,
Which perhaps is just as well because if everybody was a
    success nobody could be contemptuous of anybody else and
    everybody would start in all over again trying to be a
    bigger success than everybody else so they would have
    somebody to be contemptuous of and so on forevermore,
Because when people start hitching their wagons to a star,
That's the way they are.

Ogden Nash

Anyone can carry his burden, however hard, until nightfall.
Anyone can do his work, however hard, for one day. Anyone can
live sweetly, lovingly, purely, till the sun goes down.
And this is all that life really means.

Robert Louis Stevenson

The proper function of man is to live, not to exist. I shall not waste my days in trying to prolong them. I shall use my time.

Jack London

You will never "find" time for anything.
If you want time you must make it.

Charles Buxton

It is better to create than to be learned;
creating is the true essence of life.

Barthold Georg Niebuhr

If you will observe, it doesn't take
A man of giant mould to make
A giant shadow on the wall;
And he who in our daily sight
Seems but a figure mean and small,
Outlined in Fame's illusive light,
May stalk, a silhouette sublime
Across the canvas of his time.

J. T. Trowbridge

Dost thou love life? Then do not squander Time,
for that's the stuff life is made of.

Benjamin Franklin

If you observe a really happy man you will find him building a boat, writing a symphony, educating his son, growing double dahlias in his garden, or looking for dinosaur eggs in the Gobi desert. He will not be striving for it as a goal itself. He will have become aware that he is happy in the course of living life twenty-four crowded hours of the day.

W. Beran Wolfe

They Say

How many utterly drab and uninteresting people are there in
the world who might have developed real personalities if they had
only had the courage to do and be something different from
the crowd.

Every single forward step in history has been taken over
the bodies of empty-headed fools who giggled and snickered.

If you have anything really valuable to contribute to the world
it will come through the expression of your own personality —
that single spark of divinity that sets you off and makes you
different from every other living creature.

A noted English schoolmaster used to have as his motto:

"Never explain, never retract, never apologize. Get it done
and let them howl."

It is a motto not altogether to be commended. He who governs
his life according to it will not be an agreeable companion
or accomplish the largest service under a government where
the will of the majority must finally prevail.

But there is a rugged spirit of independence embedded in it
that many men would do well to adopt.

You can afford to have a decent regard for public opinion:
but you can never afford to let yourself get into the pathetic
condition where what "they say" or many say will keep you from
doing what ought to be done.

It is a hopeless condition to be in, because what "they say"
today is not what "they said" yesterday or "will say" tomorrow.

Bruce Barton

The art of living successfully consists of being able to hold two
opposite ideas in tension at the same time: first, to make long-term
plans as if we were going to live forever; and, second, to conduct
ourselves daily as if we were going to die tomorrow.

Sydney Harris

To be of use in this world is the only way to be happy.

Hans Christian Andersen

The difference between perseverance and obstinacy is, that one comes from a strong will, and the other from a strong won't.

Henry Ward Beecher

The world is moving so fast these days that the man who says it can't be done is generally interrupted by someone doing it.

Elbert Hubbard

A young and impressionable moth once set his heart on a certain star. He told his mother about this and she counselled him to set his heart on a bridge lamp instead. "Stars aren't the thing to hang around," she said; "lamps are the thing to hang around." "You get somewhere that way," said the moth's father. "You don't get anywhere chasing stars." But the moth would not heed the words of either parent. Every evening at dusk when the star came out he would start flying toward it and every morning at dawn he would crawl back home worn out with his vain endeavor. One day his father said to him, "You haven't burned a wing in months, boy, and it looks to me as if you were never going to. All your brothers have been badly burned flying around street lamps and all your sisters have been terribly singed flying around house lamps. Come on, now, get out of here and get yourself scorched! A big strapping moth like you without a mark on him!"

The moth left his father's house, but he would not fly around house lamps. He went right on trying to reach the star, which was four and one-third light years, or twenty-five trillion miles away. The moth thought it was just caught in the top branches of an elm. He never did reach the star, but he went right on trying, night after night.

James Thurber

There is nothing more to be esteemed than a manly firmness
and decision of character. I like a person who knows his own mind
and sticks to it; who sees at once what, in given circumstances,
is to be done, and does it.

William Hazlitt

Perseverance is a great element of success. If you only knock
long enough and loud enough at the gate, you are sure to wake
up somebody.

Henry Wadsworth Longfellow

The youth gets together his materials to build a bridge to the
moon, and, at length, the middle-aged man concludes to build a
woodshed with them.

Henry David Thoreau

Earth is Enough

We men of Earth have here the stuff
Of Paradise — we have enough!
We need no other thing to build
The stairs into the Unfulfilled —
No other ivory for the doors —
No other marble for the floors —
No other cedar for the beam
And dome of man's immortal dream.
Here on the paths of everyday —
Here on the common human way
Is all the stuff the gods would take
To build a Heaven, to mold and make
New Edens. Ours the stuff sublime
To build Eternity in Time!

Edwin Markham

Finish each day and be done with it. . . . You have done what you could; some blunders and absurdities no doubt crept in; forget them as soon as you can. Tomorrow is a new day; you shall begin it well and serenely.

Ralph Waldo Emerson

Do not wait for extraordinary circumstances to do good actions: try to use ordinary situations.

Jean Paul Richter

Whatsoever thy hand findeth to do, do it with thy might.

Ecclesiastes 9:10

Every one has a fair turn to be as great as he pleases.

Jeremy Collier

It is the greatest of all mistakes to do nothing because you can only do a little. Do what you can.

Sydney Smith

I have never been bored an hour in my life. I get up every morning wondering what new strange glamorous thing is going to happen and it happens at fairly regular intervals. Lady Luck has been good to me and I fancy she has been good to every one. Only some people are dour, and when she gives them the come hither with her eyes, they look down or turn away and lift an eyebrow. But me, I give her the wink and away we go.

William Allen White

I would rather lose in a cause that I know some day will triumph than to triumph in a cause that I know some day will fail.

Wendell L. Willkie

The man who rows the boat generally
doesn't have time to rock it.

Unknown

The mintage of wisdom is to know that rest is rust and that
the real life is love, laughter, and work.

Elbert Hubbard

The most drastic and usually the most
effective remedy for fear is direct action.

William Burnham

Live all you can; it's a mistake not to. It doesn't so much matter
what you do in particular so long as you have your life. If you
haven't had that what *have* you had?

Henry James

The great pleasure in life is doing what people say you cannot do.

Walter Bagehot

There will always be something that we shall wish
to have finished and be nevertheless unwilling to begin.

Samuel Johnson

The journey of a thousand miles begins with one step.

Lao-Tsze

Teach me your mood, O patient stars!
Who climb each night the ancient sky,
He fails alone who feebly creeps;
He wins who dares the hero's march.

Park Benjamin

None Goes His Way Alone

There is a destiny that makes us brothers:
  None goes his way alone;
All that we send into the lives of others
  Comes back into our own.

Edwin Markham

What do we live for, if it is not to make life less difficult
for each other?

George Eliot

The one essential thing is that we strive to have light in ourselves.
Our strivings will be recognized by others, and when people
have light in themselves, it will shine out from them. Then we get
to know each other as we walk together in the darkness,
without needing to pass our hands over each other's faces, or to
intrude into each other's hearts.

Albert Schweitzer

Grief can take care of itself, but to get the full value of a joy
you must have somebody to divide it with.

Mark Twain

Love has no other desire but to fulfill itself. To melt and be like
a running brook that sings its melody to the night. To wake at dawn
with a winged heart and give thanks for another day of loving.

Kahlil Gibran

I expect to pass through this world but once. Any good therefore
that I can do or any kindness that I can show for any fellow creature,
let me do it now. Let me not defer or neglect it, for I shall not pass
this way again.

Ralph Waldo Emerson

It is unfortunately only too clear that if the individual is not truly regenerated in spirit, society cannot be either, for society is the sum total of individuals in need of redemption.

C. G. Jung

Wind, Sand and Stars

We forget that there is no hope of joy except in human relations. If I draw up the balance sheet of the hours in my life that have truly counted, surely I find only those that no wealth could have procured me. True riches cannot buy friendship of a companion to whom one is bound forever by ordeals suffered in common. It is not money that can procure for us that new vision of the world won through hardship — those trees, flowers, women, those treasures made fresh by the dew and color of life which the dawn restores to us, this concert of little things that sustain us and constitute our compensation.

Nor that night we lived through in the land of the unconquered tribes of the Sahara, which now floats into my memory.

Three airplane crews had come down on the Rio de Oro coast in a part of the Sahara whose denizens acknowledge no European rule. Riguelle had landed first, with a broken connecting rod. Bourgat had come along to pick up Riguelle's crew, but a minor accident had nailed him to earth. Finally, as night was beginning to fall, I arrived. We decided to salvage Bourgat's ship but we had to spend the night and do the job of repair by daylight.

Exactly on this spot two of our comrades had been murdered by the tribesmen a year earlier. We knew that a raiding party of three hundred rifles was at this very moment encamped somewhere nearby, round Cape Bojador. Our three landings had been visible from a great distance and the Moors must have seen us. We began a vigil which might turn out to be our last.

Altogether, there were about ten of us, pilots and mechanics, when we made ready for the night. We unloaded five or six wooden cases of merchandise out of the hold, emptied them, and set them about in a circle. At the deep end of each case, as in a sentry-box, we set a lighted candle, its flame poorly sheltered from the wind. So in the heart of the desert, on the naked rind of the planet, in an isolation like that of the beginnings of the world, we built a village of men.

Sitting in the flickering light of the candles on this kerchief of sand, on this village square, we waited in the night. We were waiting for the rescuing dawn — or for the Moors. Something, I know not what, lent this night a savor of Christmas. We told stories, we joked, we sang songs. In the air there was that slight fever that reigns over a gaily prepared feast. And yet we were infinitely poor. Wind, sand, and stars. The austerity of Trappists. But on this badly lighted cloth, a handful of men who possessed nothing in the world but their memories were sharing invisible riches.

We had met at last. Men travel side by side for years, each locked up in his own silence or exchanging those words which carry no freight — till danger comes. Then they stand shoulder to shoulder. They discover that they belong to the same family. They wax and bloom in the recognition of fellow beings. They look at one another and smile. They are like the prisoner set free who marvels at the immensity of the sea.

These prison walls that this age of trade has built up around us, we can break down. We can still run free, call to our comrades, and marvel to hear once more, in response to our call, the pathetic chant of the human voice.

Antoine de Saint-Exupéry

The purpose of life is not to be happy — but to matter, to be productive, to be useful, to have it make a difference that you lived at all.

Leo Rosten

Circle One

Nothing happens only once,
Nothing happens only here,
Every love that lies asleep
Wakes today another year.

Why we sailed and how we prosper
Will be sung and lived again;
All the lands repeat themselves,
Shore for shore and men for men.

Owen Dodson

Charity

In men whom men condemn as ill
I find so much of goodness still,
In men whom men pronounce divine
I find so much of sin and blot,
I do not dare to draw a line
Between the two, where God has not.

Joaquin Miller

My creed is this:
   Happiness is the only good.
   The place to be happy is here.
   The time to be happy is now.
   The way to be happy is to help make
   others so.

Robert Ingersoll

The best cure for worry, depression, melancholy, brooding, is to
sally deliberately forth and try to lift with one's sympathy the gloom
of somebody else.

Arnold Bennett

Up to a certain point it is good for us to know that there are
people in the world who will give us love and unquestioned loyalty
to the limit of their ability. I doubt, however, if it is good for us
to feel assured of this without the accompanying obligation
of having to justify their devotion by our behavior.

Eleanor Roosevelt

A person remains immature, whatever his age, as long as he thinks
of himself as an exception to the human race.

Harry Overstreet

I have believed the best of every man.
And find that to believe it is enough
To make a bad man show him at his best,
Or even a good man swing his lantern higher.

William Butler Yeats

I believe that we can live on earth according to the teachings of
Jesus, and that the greatest happiness will come to the world when
man obeys His commandment "Love ye one another."

I believe that we can live on earth according to the fulfillment of
God's will, and that when the will of God is done on earth as
it is done in heaven, every man will love his fellow men, and act
towards them as he desires they should act towards him. I believe
that the welfare of each is bound up in the welfare of all.

I believe that life is given us so we may grow in love, and I believe
that God is in me as the sun is in the color and fragrance of a
flower — the Light in my darkness, the Voice in my silence.

I believe that only in broken gleams has the Sun of Truth yet
shone upon men. I believe that love will finally establish the
Kingdom of God on earth, and that the Cornerstones of that
Kingdom will be Liberty, Truth, Brotherhood, and Service.

Helen Keller

I will not permit any man to narrow and degrade my soul
by making me hate him.

Booker T. Washington

Maturing is the process by which the individual becomes conscious
of the equal importance of each of his fellow men.

Alvin Goeser

To get rid of an enemy, one must love him.

Leo Tolstoy

A great many people think they are thinking when they are merely
rearranging their prejudices.

William James

Always do right. This will gratify some people, and astonish
the rest.

Mark Twain

A rattlesnake, if cornered, will become so angry it will bite itself.
That is exactly what the harboring of hate and resentment
against others is — a biting of oneself. We think that we are harming
others in holding these spites and hates, but the deeper harm
is to ourselves.

E. Stanley Jones

Outwitted

He drew a circle that shut me out —
Heretic, rebel, a thing to flout.
But Love and I had the wit to win:
We drew a circle that took him in.

Edwin Markham

You May Count That Day

If you sit down at set of sun
And count the acts that you have done
   And counting, find
One self-denying deed, one word
That eased the heart of him who heard —
   One glance most kind,
That fell like sunshine where it went
Then you may count that day well spent.

But if, through all the livelong day
You've cheered no heart, by yea or nay —
   If, through it all
You've nothing done that you can trace
That brought the sunshine to one face —
   No act most small
That helped some soul and nothing cost —
Then count that day as worse than lost.

George Eliot

Happiness is like a kiss — in order to get any good out of it
you have to give it to somebody else.

Unknown

Strong and bitter words indicate a weak cause.

Victor Hugo

When a friend asks, there is no tomorrow.

George Herbert

A man is called selfish, not for pursuing his own good, but for
neglecting his neighbor's.

Richard Whately

Man has survived everything, and we have only survived it on our optimism, and optimism means faith in ourselves, faith in the everydayness of our lives, faith in our universal qualities, and above all, faith in love.

Edward Steichen

The Things I Prize

These are the things I prize
   And hold of dearest worth:
Light of the sapphire skies,
Peace of the silent hills,
Shelter of the forests, comfort of the grass,
Music of birds, murmur of little rills,
Shadows of clouds that swiftly pass,
   And, after showers,
   The smell of flowers
And of the good brown earth —
And best of all, along the way, friendship and mirth.

Henry Van Dyke

Forgive others often, yourself never.

Publius Syrus

I am not bound to win but I am bound to be true. I am not bound to succeed but I am bound to live up to what light I have. I must stand with anybody that stands right: stand with him while he is right and part with him when he goes wrong.

Abraham Lincoln

Keep your fears to yourself,
but share your courage with others.

Robert Louis Stevenson

He who wished to secure the good of others,
has already secured his own.

Confucius

Free will, though it makes evil possible, is also the only thing
that makes possible any love of goodness or joy worth having.

C. S. Lewis

I can live for two months on a good compliment.

Mark Twain

Watch, America

Where the northern ocean darkens,
Where the rolling rivers run,
Past the cold and empty headlands,
Toward the slow and westering sun,
There our fathers, long before us,
Armed with freedom, faced the deep;
What they won with love and labor,
Let their children watch and keep.

By our dark and dreaming forests,
By our free and shining skies,
By our green and ripening prairies,
Where the western mountains rise;
God who gave our fathers freedom,
God who made our fathers brave,
What they built with love and anguish,
Let their children watch and save.

Robert Nathan

The world is a fine place and worth fighting for.

Ernest Hemingway

Friendship is almost always the union of a part of one mind with
a part of another; people are friends in spots.

George Santayana

Don't tell your friends about your indigestion:
"How are you!" is a greeting, not a question.

Arthur Guiterman

Blessed are they who have nothing to say,
and who cannot be persuaded to say it.

James Russell Lowell

When a man comes to me for advice, I find out the kind of advice
he wants and I give it to him.

Josh Billings

The most skilful flattery is to let a person
talk on, and be a listener.

Joseph Addison

What is Love? I have met in the streets a very poor young man
who was in love. His hat was old, his coat worn, the water
passed through his shoes and the stars through his soul.

Victor Hugo

He that blows the coals in a quarrel he has nothing to do with
has no right to complain if the sparks fly in his face.

Benjamin Franklin

You cannot do a kindness too soon, because
you never know how soon it will be too late.

Old Proverb

A Friend

There is no friend like an old friend
  Who has shared our morning days,
No greeting like his welcome,
  No homage like his praise.
Fame is the scentless flower,
  With gaudy crown of gold;
But friendship is the breathing rose,
  With sweets in every fold.

Oliver Wendell Holmes

One man with courage makes a majority.

Andrew Jackson

There are no rules for friendship. It must be left to itself.
We cannot force it any more than love.

William Hazlitt

All we can do is to make the best of our friends, love and cherish
what is good in them, and keep out of the way of what is bad.

Thomas Jefferson

To be popular at home is a great achievement. The man who is
loved by the house cat, by the dog, by the neighbor's children,
and by his own wife, is a great man, even if he has never had his
name in Who's Who.

Thomas Dreier

Man is a special being, and if left to himself, in an isolated
condition, would be one of the weakest creatures; but associated
with his kind, he works wonders.

Daniel Webster

I Dream a World

I Dream A World

I dream a world where man
No other will scorn,
Where love will bless the earth
And peace its paths adorn.
I dream a world where all
Will know sweet freedom's way,
Where greed no longer saps the soul
Nor avarice blights our day.
A world I dream where black or white,
Whatever race you be,
Will share the bounties of the earth
And every man is free,
Where wretchedness will hang its head,
And joy, like a pearl,
Attend the needs of all mankind.
Of such I dream —
Our world!

Langston Hughes

Have courage for the great sorrow of life and patience for the
small one; and when you have laboriously accomplished your daily
task, go to sleep in peace. God is awake.

Victor Hugo

I looked more widely around me. I studied the lives of the masses
of humanity, and I saw that, not two or three, or ten, but hundreds,
thousands, millions, had so understood the meaning of life
that they were able both to live and to die. All these men were
well acquainted with the meaning of life and death, quietly labored,
endured privation and suffering, lived and died, and saw in
all this, not a vain, but a good thing.

Leo Tolstoy

That all the jarring notes of life
  Seem blending in a psalm,
And all the angles of its strife
  Slow rounding into calm.

And so the shadows fall apart,
  And so the west-winds play;
And all the windows of my heart
  I open to the day.

John Greenleaf Whittier

Life was meant to be lived, and curiosity must be kept alive.
One must never, for whatever reason, turn his back on life.

Eleanor Roosevelt

For Joy

For each and every joyful thing,
For twilight swallows on the wing,
For all that nests and all that sings —

For fountains cool that laugh and leap,
For rivers running to the deep,
For happy, care-forgetting sleep,—

For stars that pierce the sombre dark,
For Morn, awaking with the lark,
For life new-stirring 'neath the bark,—

For sunshine and the blessed rain,
For budding grove and blossoming lane,
For the sweet silence of the plain,—

For bounty springing from the sod,
For every step by beauty trod,—
For each dear gift of joy, thank God!

Florence Earle Coates

One of the most tragic things I know about human nature is that all of us tend to put off living. We are all dreaming of some magical rose garden over the horizon — instead of enjoying the roses that are blooming outside our windows today.

Dale Carnegie

Don't let life discourage you; everyone who got where he is had to begin where he was.

Richard L. Evans

Your World

Your world is as big as you make it.
I know, for I used to abide
In the narrowest nest in a corner,
My wings pressing close to my side.

But I sighted the distant horizon
Where the skyline encircled the sea
And I throbbed with a burning desire
To travel this immensity.

I battered the cordons around me
And cradled my wings on the breeze
Then soared to the uttermost reaches
With rapture, with power, with ease!

Georgia Douglas Johnson

He who defends with love will be secure; Heaven will save him, and protect him with love.

Lao-Tzu

There is no soul that does not respond to love, for the soul of man is a guest that has gone hungry these centuries back.

Maurice Maeterlinck

Write it on your heart that every day is the best day in the year.

Ralph Waldo Emerson

The future . . . seems to me no unified dream but a mince pie, long in the baking, never quite done.

E. B. White

Measurement

Stars and atoms have no size,
They only vary in men's eyes.

Men and instruments will blunder
— Calculating things of wonder.

A seed is just as huge a world
As any ball the sun has hurled.

Stars are quite as picayune
As any splinter of the moon.

Time is but a vague device;
Space can never be precise;

Stars and atoms have a girth,
Small as zero, ten times Earth.

There is, by God's swift reckoning
A universe in everything.

A. M. Sullivan

Those who attempt to search into the majesty of God will be overwhelmed with its glory.

Thomas à Kempis

The best way to know God is to love many things.

Vincent van Gogh

I am an optimist. It does not seem too much use being
anything else.

Winston Churchill

Life is something like this trumpet. If you don't put anything in it
you don't get anything out. And that's the truth.

W. C. Handy

I am convinced that my life belongs to the whole community;
and as long as I live, it is my privilege to do for it whatever I can,
for the harder I work the more I live.
    I rejoice in life for its own sake. Life is no brief candle to me.
It is a sort of splendid torch which I got hold of for a moment, and I
want to make it burn as brightly as possible before turning it
over to future generations.

George Bernard Shaw

Happiness sneaks in through a door you didn't know you left open.

John Barrymore

Look to this day! For it is life,
   The very life of life.
In its brief course lie all the varieties
And realities of your existence.
   The bliss of growth,
   The glory of action,
   The splendor of beauty,
For yesterday is but a dream,
And tomorrow is only a vision;
   But today well lived
Makes every yesterday a dream of happiness,
And every tomorrow a vision of hope.
Look well, therefore, to this day!

Unknown

The wealth of man is the number of things which he loves and blesses, which he is loved and blessed by.

Thomas Carlyle

Nothing is so strong as gentleness;
nothing so gentle as real strength.

St. Francis of Sales

The man who cannot wonder, who does not habitually wonder and worship, is but a pair of spectacles behind which there is no eye.

Thomas Carlyle

He that walketh with wise men shall be wise.

Proverbs 13:20

Truth and love are two of the most powerful things in the world; and when they both go together they cannot easily be withstood.

Ralph Cudworth

Have hope. Though clouds environ round
   And gladness hides her face in scorn,
Put off the shadow from thy brow;
   No night but hath its morn.

Have faith. Where'er thy bark is driven —
   The calm's disport, the tempest's mirth —
Know this: God rules the hosts of heaven,
   The inhabitants of earth.

Have love. Not love alone for one,
   But man, as man, thy brother call;
And scatter, like a circling sun,
   Thy charities on all.

Friedrich von Schiller

Resolved to live with all my might while I do live, and as I shall
wish I had done ten thousand years hence.

Jonathan Edwards

The ignorant man marvels at the exceptional;
the wise man marvels at the common.

George Boardman

God must have loved the plain people:
He made so many of them.

Abraham Lincoln

Don't part with your illusions. When they are gone you may still
exist but you have ceased to live.

Mark Twain

Night

Stars over snow,
   And in the west a planet
Swinging below a star —
   Look for a lovely thing and you will find it,
It is not far —
   It never will be far.

Sara Teasdale

Fulfill something you are able to fulfill, rather than run after
what you will never achieve. Nobody is perfect. Remember the
saying "None is good but God alone." And nobody can be.
It is an illusion. We can modestly strive to fulfill ourselves and to
be as complete human beings as possible, and that will give us
trouble enough.

C. G. Jung

"One can't believe impossible things." "I daresay you haven't had much practice," said the Queen. "When I was your age, I always did it for half-an-hour a day. Why, sometimes I've believed as many as six impossible things before breakfast."

Lewis Carroll

Enjoy your own life without comparing it with that of another.

Marquis de Condorcet

When love and skill work together, expect a masterpiece.

John Ruskin

Happiness doesn't come from doing what we like to do but from liking what we have to do.

Wilfred Peterson

With a Bunch of Roses

Here's last year's grief
In the green leaf;

And all he knows is
That Time will take
All Heartbreak,
And turn it to roses.

Robert Nathan

Happiness makes up in height for what it lacks in length.

Robert Frost

The world is round and the place which may seem like the end may also be only the beginning.

Ivy Baker Priest

We thank Thee for this place in which we dwell, for the love that unites us, for the peace accorded us this day, for hope with which we expect the morrow, for the health, the work, the food and the bright skies that make our life delightful; for our friends in all parts of the earth. Spare to us our friends, soften to us our enemies. Bless us if it may be in all our innocent endeavors. If it may not, give us strength to encounter that which is to come that we may be brave in peril, constant in tribulation, temperate in wrath and in all changes of fortune, and down to the gates of death, loyal and loving one to another . . .

Robert Louis Stevenson

The truth is that life is delicious, horrible, charming, frightful, sweet, bitter, and that it is everything.

Anatole France

Credo

I cannot find my way: there is no star
In all the shrouded heavens anywhere:
And there is not a whisper in the air
Of any living voice but one so far
That I can hear it only as a bar
Of lost, imperial music, played when fair
And angel fingers wove, and unaware,
Dead leaves to garlands where no roses are.

No, there is not a glimmer, nor a call,
For one that welcomes, welcomes when he fears,
The black and awful chaos of the night;
For through it all — above, beyond it all —
I know the far-sent message of the years,
I feel the coming glory of the Light.

Edwin Arlington Robinson

If one advances confidently in the direction of his dreams, and endeavors to live the life which he has imagined, he will meet with a success unexpected in common hours . . . If you have built castles in the air, your work need not be lost; that is where they should be. Now put foundations under them.

Henry David Thoreau

I begin to suspect that a man's bewilderment is the measure of his wisdom.

Nathaniel Hawthorne

The value of experience is not in seeing much but in seeing wisely.

Sir William Osler

All things are possible to him that believeth.

Mark 9:23

Acceptance

When the spent sun throws up its rays on cloud
And goes down burning into the gulf below,
No voice in nature is heard to cry aloud
At what has happened. Birds, at least, must know
It is the change to darkness in the sky.
Murmuring something quiet in her breast,
One bird begins to close a faded eye;
Or overtaken too far from his nest,
Hurrying low above the grove, some waif
Swoops just in time to his remembered tree.
At most he thinks or twitters softly, "Safe!
Now let the night be dark for all of me.
Let the night be too dark for me to see
Into the future. Let what will be, be."

Robert Frost

Common-sense in an uncommon degree is what the world calls wisdom.

Samuel Taylor Coleridge

Is it so small a thing to have enjoyed the sun, to have lived light in the spring, to have loved, to have thought, to have done?

Matthew Arnold

Resolve to see the world on the sunny side, and you have almost won the battle of life at the outset.

Sir Roger L'Estrange

Beauty is so precious, the enjoyments it gives are so refined and pure, so congenial with our tenderest and noblest feelings, and so akin to worship, that it is painful to think of the multitude of men as living in the midst of it, and living almost as blind to it as if, instead of the fair earth and glorious sky, they were living in a dungeon.

William Channing

When I would beget content and increase confidence in the power and wisdom and providence of Almighty God, I will walk the meadows by some gliding stream, and there contemplate the lilies that take no care, and those very many other little living creatures that are not only created, but fed (man knows not how) by the goodness of the God of Nature, and therefore trust in Him.

Izaak Walton

Every great and commanding moment in the annals of the world is the triumph of some enthusiasm.

Ralph Waldo Emerson

Acknowledgments

The editor and the publisher have made every effort to trace the ownership of all copyrighted material and to secure permission from holders of such material. In the event of any question arising as to the use of any material the publisher and editor, while expressing regret for inadvertent error, will be pleased to make the necessary corrections in future printings. Thanks are due to the following authors, publishers, publications and agents for permission to use the material indicated.

D. APPLETON-CENTURY CROFTS, INC., for "They Say" from *Better Days* by Bruce Barton.

ATHENEUM PUBLISHERS, INC., for "Leavetaking" by Eve Merriam from *It Doesn't Always Have To Rhyme,* copyright 1962 by Eve Merriam; and "A Lazy Thought" by Eve Merriam from *There Is No Rhyme for Silver,* copyright 1962 by Eve Merriam.

MRS. DOROTHY CHESTON BENNETT, for a quotation by Arnold Bennett.

THE BOBBS-MERRILL COMPANY, INC., for lines from *A Fortune To Share* by Vash Young, copyright 1931 and renewed 1959 by Vash Young.

THE CANDLELIGHT PRESS, INC., for "April" from *Intent on Earth* by Marcia Lee Masters, copyright 1965 by Marcia Lee Masters Schmid.

CITADEL PRESS, INC., for lines from *The Spiritual Sayings of Kahlil Gibran.*

COLLINS PUBLISHERS, for extracts from *The Case for Christianity* by C. S. Lewis.

DOUBLEDAY AND COMPANY, INC., for paragraphs from *Midstream* by Helen Keller, copyright 1929 by Helen Keller and The Crowell Publishing Company.

CONSTANCE GARLAND DOYLE and ISABEL GARLAND LORD for "Do You Fear the Wind" by Hamlin Garland.

E. P. DUTTON & COMPANY, INC., for 10 lines from *Raccoons Are the Brightest People* by Sterling North, copyright 1966 by Sterling North.

MRS. MAX EASTMAN for selection from *Enjoyment of Laughter* by Max Eastman.

EPOS, for "Wonder Wander" by Lenore Kandel from Summer, 1961, issue of Epos.

A. M. SULLIVAN, for "Measurement" from *Stars and Atoms Have No Size.*

MRS. JAMES THURBER, for "The Moth and the Star" from *Fables For Our Time* by James Thurber, copyright 1940 by James Thurber, published by Harper and Row. (Originally printed in *The New Yorker*); for a selection in "Sex Ex Machina" from *Let Your Mind Alone,* by James Thurber, copyright 1937 by James Thurber, copyright 1965 by Helen W. Thurber and Rosemary Thurber Savers, published by Harper and Row (Originally printed in *The New Yorker*). To Hamish Hamilton, for the same selections from *Vintage Thurber* by James Thurber, copyright 1963.

A. P. WATT & SON for quotations from the works of Rudyard Kipling, H. G. Wells and Ogden Nash.

WM. H. WISE & COMPANY, INC., Publishers, for two selections from *Philistine* by Elbert Hubbard.

THE WORLD PUBLISHING COMPANY, for a selection from *What This World Needs* by John Raper, copyright 1954 by The World Publishing Company.